DEAN BROWNE is from County Tipperary and currently lives in Cork. He received the Geoffrey Dearmer Prize in 2021. His chapbook *Kitchens at Night* was a winner of the Poetry Business International Pamphlet Competition, and published by Smith|Doorstop in 2022. *After Party* is his first collection.

ALSO BY DEAN BROWNE

Kitchens at Night

Dean Browne

After Party

PICADOR

First published 2025 by Picador
an imprint of Pan Macmillan
The Smithson, 6 Briset Street, London EC1M 5NR
EU representative: Macmillan Publishers Ireland Ltd, 1st Floor,
The Liffey Trust Centre, 117–126 Sheriff Street Upper,
Dublin 1 D01 YC43
Associated companies throughout the world

ISBN 978-1-0350-5467-1

Copyright © Dean Browne 2025

The right of Dean Browne to be identified as the
author of this work has been asserted in accordance with
the Copyright, Designs and Patents Act 1988.

All rights reserved. No part of this publication may be reproduced,
stored in a retrieval system, or transmitted, in any form, or by any means
(including, without limitation, electronic, mechanical, photocopying, recording
or otherwise) without the prior written permission of the publisher.

Pan Macmillan does not have any control over, or any responsibility for,
any author or third-party websites (including, without limitation, URLs,
emails and QR codes) referred to in or on this book.

1 3 5 7 9 8 6 4 2

A CIP catalogue record for this book is available from the British Library.

Printed and bound by CPI Group (UK) Ltd, Croydon CR0 4YY

This book is sold subject to the condition that it shall not, by way of trade or otherwise, be lent, hired out, or otherwise circulated without the publisher's prior consent in any form of binding or cover other than that in which it is published and without a similar condition including this condition being imposed on the subsequent purchaser. The publisher does not authorize the use or reproduction of any part of this book in any manner for the purpose of training artificial intelligence technologies or systems. The publisher expressly reserves this book from the Text and Data Mining exception in accordance with Article 4(3) of the European Union Digital Single Market Directive 2019/790.

Visit **www.picador.com** to read more about all our books and to buy them.

To whom then am I addressed?
To the imagination.

WILLIAM CARLOS WILLIAMS

Contents

Aide-Mémoire 1
Shadow Box 2
Rachael's Coat Inside Out 4
Scuttle 5
Flinch 6
Today I Want to Miss Only My Favourite Shoes of All Time 7
Pinball 9
Spacer 10
To Félicette 12
Butternut Squash 14
Oink 16
From the Basement Tapes 17
Anniversary 20
The Leg 21
The Triangle 23
Days of the Brindled Cow 24
It Cannot Be Salvaged 26
Fascinators 27
Barmbrack 28
Small Yellow Spider 29
Pine Box in the Flea Market 30
Polyphemus 32
Interval (in which, snow) 33

Listening to Joni Mitchell's *Blue* While Cooking Peposo   34
Notes Toward an Epithalamium   35
Pine Box in the Flea Market   36
A Cigarette   37
Tabernacle   38
The Infinite   39
Prayer to Buster Keaton   40
Approach to an Egg   41
Horse Chestnuts   42
Quiche   44
My Last Consultation   45
Parachuting into the Volcano   47
The Pineapple Massage   48
Synastry Chart   49
Approach to Chilli   50
The Cup   51
Flies   52
Percy French   53
Afternaut   54
Self-Checkout   56
Reverb   57
Party After The The   59
The Goatfish   60
As if, A Land Called   61

Notes   63
Acknowledgements   65

After Party

Aide-Mémoire

A goat has been following me for hours. There is a sign
hung around his neck that reads NEVER FORGET.
That's not very original I think but I'll see where it leads.
'I have no grá for you goat', I say, and clap my hands, say, 'Go!'
His goat eye asks if I am half-cracked. 'Grand', I say,
and keep walking. He follows at a discreet distance, beard
jigging crooked as he jaws blankly at some grass he cropped
years ago, I suppose. What am I meant to remember?
Leaves are smeared on the street, a salad of dragged newspaper.
Nobody appears to notice what is following me. I detour
into a dive bar, roll a cigarette, drink a double whiskey
and try to decide where, if anywhere, all this might connect.
Goat stands by the door, NEVER FORGET dripping to the tiles.
I watch wet leaves fibrillate outside the window, think
of the small, delicate feather on this morning's egg. Leaf, light,
leaf, light. Quick silverfish glimpses of a freedom that spooks
on approach. The goat chews on, relentless. I mash my cigarette,
touch my ear, and it comes off.

Shadow Box

So this is the after party
our cherished stuff attends
when we're gone.
A draughty, sunless place.

The hours you'll lose
in this carnival
of corners, and not clock
what you're after!

But you know, between
such linty chintz
and shadows
it will suggest itself.

You inhale fathers
of tobacco-smoke from suede.
Your foot snags on a dress
as though it pleaded –

it might have been
stitched by a miniaturist
from stray histories
quilting waste ground.

The piled strata
of vinyl, the defaced sleeves
composing ring on ring
a family tree of sorts.

Not heaven, this
whistling vacuum in space,
lives shunted to the side,
a price tag in biro.

Suspended here
in its topheavy, lopsided
geometry –
a walk-in shadow box –

the platoon of gooseneck
lamps at oblique angles,
the poignancy of a hedge-
hog posed in brass.

A bald doll looking down
from its circle, one eye
turned back into the skull,
fixed on the future. Yours.

Rachael's Coat Inside Out

It's floating on a wire hanger now
from the lowest branch in a corner
of the forest. You unhook it,
thumbs worrying stitches for what
you missed last time in the dark
shifty material lining the interior –
the slit left by a torn-away button,
burns, the nervous designs of moths
flickering in and out at the collar.
Your dreams make all kinds of no sense –
locked cabinets with cobwebs across
the wobbly glass knobs. Rachael
adjusts on her nothing shoulders
the winter coat she'd have worn,
the stitching so gone in the pockets
her hands believe they're bottomless.
She could keep a rat in one, the teeth,
the pink loop of tail, brush against us
this close, and who would even know
what she carried there?

Scuttle

I'm somewhere I shouldn't be.
Eight, allergic to dust,
asthmatic, stigmatic
with mystery rashes,
balanced tiptoe on a stack
of peat briquettes
wound in butcher's twine,
fingers smutty from
Suttons Premium Polish Coal.
In that bungalow
shadowed by mountain, things
clenched past function –
blunt tools, used batteries.
Hand-me-down grudges.
Where do you dispose of them,
old keys? One's blue-green
brass with smoky thumb stain,
chunky, no discernible fit
with anything begun since me.
Layabouts could scan clouds
in that pinhole in its head.
This memory flukes through it.
And I press the edge,
the teeth, till it hurts.

Flinch

The dead, they're scattered everyway under, like a knocked-over
 toybox.
I can't put a foot right.

Of course I don't feel them like an upturned plug
forking a bare sole, a quick, bloodless shock

in the dark of the landing, for example.
And why there? There's not even a socket close to there.

Today I Want to Miss Only My Favourite Shoes of All Time

More akin to ousted nestlings now
than brogues, the laceless caramel suede
withered scrotal. Once, daylight was kinder,

bouncing back off the polished toecaps. Cloudlike,
cushioning low arches nicely. I felt handsome,
airborne. The sex.

My spirit, iridescent organza.
Should have enshrined them. I stormed them
into French onion soup

weather too often, they went the way of all things
beautiful: wore up one side,
the wet seeped in.

Whatever craft joined the sole steadfast
degraded, came unglued.
You must imagine them reduced

to a flipflop smackety-smack against
the path's dodgy pop-up flags.
I thought of the deep-fried sleaze of chitterlings

killed on the cusp of fun-loving.
Thought of beachcombers in oilskins
liberating from the sand and wrack

these two buffeted currachs
that returned as skeletal relics west.
My various travels strewn

for dissection on the cobbler's bench
like stunned bats

any second to flap wild about the room.

Pinball

He let the oxygen mask slip
from the crow's nest of stubble
so I leant in closer, to catch
that he didn't want a headstone –
no wings, no spidery gothic script –
instead, an old pinball machine
should mark the place of his grave.
He liked the plink under his thumbs;
he talked bumpers, flippers, kickers,
forbidden tilts, 'shooting for the moon',
how a ball knocked out of bounds
might come back, Lazarus, and win.
I saw tournaments among the tombs,
a horsebox paused by the fresh earth,
a generator, set up to the side
under that knuckle of hill in Donegal.
He inserts the first cold coins
by the yew trees, under the moon,
pulls the plunger – flashing outlanes
bop and spark against the marble,
focusing names and dates,
gilt epitaphs, and stone angels
watching hi-scores rack up.
I know before the night is out
his initials will join the wizards'.

Spacer

Orphaned young, giving up on love
before it gave up on him, bluesman Byther Smith
approaches NASA, keen to be
First Man to Play the Blues on the Moon.
It would be a homecoming. He couldn't skirt
the maternal aspect of that satellite.
Escapist much? the arch rejoinder came.
Even space exploration has its coffee hour –
nobody was more surprised than me
to uncover archival evidence
thanks to the tethered space photographers,
albeit all skewed angles, moon-debris.
Space being airless, how'd he get the juice
for the tune, where all sound halts? A problem
for engineers. But a studio was installed
on the lunar surface, half a kilometre
or so from the flag; the astronauts
beamed Byther up with his Silvertone.
There are 128 Hawaiian bobtail squids in orbit
currently, why not one blues guitarist?
Down here, with ragwort and crabgrass
under my window open to moonless drizzle,
I turn the dial to static. One whisper of
groove should reach my hopelessly sublunar ears,
the infested hush between frequencies,
that might be him, long-fingered virtuosic

fosterling of the moon, in the incredible
heavens; his hoped-for excursion
six decades on, transmitted to this street.

To Félicette

The French did you dirty, Félicette.
Scooped you up from the scrappy, unneutered boulevards
where you'd spat at a cabal of horny toms

or sullied the white socks of your luscious
flea-ridden tux
lapping, with relish, rancid leftovers in the backstreets

of bistros, letting the busboy scratch you behind the ear,
or pinning, for fun, a butterfly under your paw,
with the moon at the correct distance.

An arrogant purpose attended your capture
not even your potent nose, your vigilant instinct
for danger could have divined.

Even now I can just see your distressed shedding
and the lit black of your eyes
as those moonmen handle you dispassionately

as a specimen upon which to experiment,
implanting their electrodes, graphing your impulses.
Forget them, Félicette. 'C 341' is no name

and 'Felix' misgendered you, love,
and aboard the Véronique AG1 rocket ship
as the payload disarticulates –

parachute or no – is no place for a cat,
one, like you, particularly lovely,
particularly liable to be let filch a bit of Gruyère

or, abristle with need for affection or feeding
to step blithely on the heads of sleepers,
to nudge them awake.

What can I say, Félicette? The moon is an ossuary
and its valentines have chilly ways.
I'm glad those Frenchmen learned sweet fuck all

when they prodded your brain, old girl – could dream
only you, for a moment, in space, weightless,
and what you saw, took with you.

Butternut Squash

Well if it isn't the Venus of Willendorf –
upright on the kitchen countertop,
plump pastel gourd in its zone
returning the illumination it receives.
Closer, more tanned than pastel – ecru?
Cousinly to pumpkin but more demure.
I approach, hands lost at my sides, chest tight,
rotundity not unbecoming an arse
bared in this tricky, partial light.
But it's not arses I'm thinking of
when the lopped-off top and bottom
ends go frisbee to the compost bin;
my hands move in, shaving hard rind,
past that clandestine, second rind to
the blood orange weather unexpressed there –
no, rather how the farther I travel in
the more must be disposed –
divided, its pulpy breach of seeds
and intricacy of tangles I teaspoon loose,
this painstaking little process
of surgery and sunburst!
I'm sorry to lose so much.
There were details I failed to list
in all the sad inadequate apartments
we rented successively – now
a hillock of loose peels I sweep aside.

Schoolfriends, what's-his-name
and how it felt to slide shoeless on
the cherrywood floor of a childhood
bedroom. Only a fool refuses to believe
in ghosts. I am cubing the squash
as precisely as I can, as if
somewhere it's not too late
to describe these things. To try.

Oink

We were so poor we fried eggs on a spoon.

I held it steady over the candleflame in a cupboard sublet by the butcher.

First of the month he clomped upstairs, eye ringed like the bottom of a coffee cup.

One day he pulled from his apron a pig's ear, for me to play with.

My mother bit her nails back to the elbow.

I pressed it to the floor. I pressed it to the wall. I didn't need a boost to press it to the ceiling.

'Mind now', the mother laughed with her nerves.

But I was happy snouting in spider webs and old scrunched-up bills, bills, bills. A smell of wild thyme. I ploughed a furrow in rubbish hunting for truffles.

I couldn't hear her anymore.

I was strung up by my trotters. The room grew smaller, shrunk to a fly's bloody footprint. My backbone cried with the weight of me. Sawdust.

An enamel bucket   blubbed.

The butcher tickled under my chin, 'poor child', just where the wound was.

From the Basement Tapes

Brian, I'm still calling you Brian,
it's raining and Sunday where you gig
now, or it isn't. I can only reconstruct

you from the stickers, scabbed
and bleaching on the punished body
of your gnarly Tanglewood.

The nurse reattached your fingertip
but a wallop from the yard brush
ruptured your eardrum.

One less ear for tinnitus to fuck,
you'd smirk, no polished savant you
but your hands were charmed.

You'd oblige when a haze of stragglers
at the party passed the toy ukulele,
pluck until the big fella wept.

Ais, moonlighting as a dilettante
astrologer for pub money, saw collisions
in your nativity, tapping an ochre nail

on your tenth house of fame
in the horoscope she'd drawn in air
and that cinched it.

One time you said we'd tour Egypt.
But Brian I've pawned my tinny amp
and the Stratocaster wasn't mine to keep.

Story with rent? Even a frontman
of your cut and *sacrée tignasse*
might be turfed out on a landlord's whim.

But I know the story. Or I do its gist.
The scraggly contours. Box bedroom. Skint.
Don't ask me how, but I feel

some tomorrow your name will occur
and I'll shrug no news since this.
I'll wish I asked then, 'Why Egypt?'

Maybe don't wade out so far alone
some beautiful day in June
until the sound stops.

Just square this as a crappy phase
of the moon's twenty-and-eight.
I want tortoiseshell plectrums for you.

Whisht, is what you say, a querying thumb
jabbed in the direction of the bar
where the tune is jangling down.

You know what it is.
You've heard it before, you think — where?
It's not my place to say.

Anniversary

Another blast of confetti
from the parade float, bunting
from some one-shop village
with a church, called Kilmuck.

Local occasion commemorating
one or other of the helpless rabbits
history bloods its lurchers on.
Laughing boy on dad's shoulders,

mother withdrawn and scrolling.
For three nights the sandman
has bivouacked elsewhere
and tendered barely a grain,

the country doctor's flummoxed.
*Does it hurt when I press here
or here or here? Have you anyone
else to chat to about this?*

*Well, that's your choice.
Wouldn't recommend it.*
And *How's Cormac getting on?
I sat the Leaving with him.*

The Leg

As children we were told
how the train door unexpectedly
shut, the wheels began to turn,
separating the man from his leg.
I'd imagine the leg travelling
on the train, away from the rest
of him, reducing to a red dot
on the platform, under cool eyes
that lifted, with a flap, into the sky.
What did the leg see out the window?
Cows likely, lots of rushy fields,
furze flowering on the mountain
like a bruise, the fat blackberries
tarring the air, shiny as videotape
in the stickly, unforgiving ditches.
The tale was meant to point
a warning, I'm sure – *no playing
near the railway tracks* –
but I put in work on the pillow,
and there goes the leg, journeying
past the abandoned creamery
slashed with the brambles of
my grandmother's memory,
past Thurles, past Portlaoise even.
Last I heard the leg was living
comfortably on the coast
of France. Stamps are a hobby

and a glass of the local grape
will see postcards written, unwritten,
thrown in the sea, where it stands
a long time, then stutters back up shore.

The Triangle

I should never have written the instruction manual
illustrating the 52 distinct tones that can be struck
from the triangle, popular now in concert halls
from here to Berlin. It's brought me nothing but success.

The joke, at first, was exquisite as a devilled egg
and the expression on their faces like a sweet pimento.
You put the phony in symphony tonight, grinned back
the shiny hand-dryer in the gents. Gobs dropped

and I went on, describing the point tapped just so
for the blackbird's dawn trill, the ripple on a clear lake
in Sweden, the squeak of gas that jets from a roasting coal.
One tone only audible to toddlers, another only to dogs.

Of course I reddened when those rich fools googled me,
the search results proved it true. The hits were legion.
Not only that, the book had entered its fourth print run
and was forthcoming in Russian and Nynorsk.

That's when it occurred to me that I was late
to deliver the keynote address at the annual summit
for triangle-lovers, my lecture on the sweeter octaves
of beryllium copper – how to damp it for the rustle

like the train of a bridal dress over cobbles.
Or pitch it like the mice celebrating the owl's demise
by lightning. Or the *ting!* so crystalline it's called 'frost creeping'.
So I jotted some notes, grabbed my jacket, and said *taxi*.

Days of the Brindled Cow

It's my neighbour Eli running over the road in the rain
with a litre of milk. It's my neighbour Eli running over.
It's the road either side of the milk raining.
It's my neighbour rain running home with a litre of Eli.
Birds peel away in patterns that look arbitrary.
Birds against the tinny rose yellow of the sky.

Birds above a bleedy fingernail of horizon.
Hard-worked Eli blown away and back a birch of a man.
The windowed children watch, their numbed mothers
tinker with the blinds, long nails greyed to the beds
from picking at scratchcards. The horizon bleeding
into the birds. Eli dripping from a wing of horizon.

He's a part-time projectionist at the cinema in town,
through misty beams he sees – new specs Eli –
the backs of heads breaching in a sea of shadows,
which seems more and more the story, not the screen.
If the stories lack salt they stir up their own.
This month's crazy unlucky for me, it's sabotage!
he says into the wing of his saturated jacket

and simply dissolves. Rain bamboozles his innermost.
It's that story he tells himself about the weather that means
himself. Dear Eli, if I drove I'd fling open the door
on the passenger side. It's my neighbour nobody now
horizoning over the wings. He's on the bird road home.
It's my road running over Eli in the milk with a litre
of litre. A story either side of Eli that keeps raining roads.

It Cannot Be Salvaged

Make me scrambled eggs,
she never said.
I will so, I said,
and never did.

Fascinators

The bridesmaids have gone paintballing
their cloudy plumage lines the street outside
the ha-ha of enchant and garble's what
a strange ear hears them criss and cross.

Their cloudy plumage lines the street outside
sloughed off in spate, like geese, like anchored ghosts.
A strange ear hears them criss and cross:
'Do ye say it like lichens or lichens . . . ?'

Sloughed off in spate, like geese, or anchored ghosts
they grew tired of being chatted up.
Do I say it like lichens or lichens?
I says that gate could do with some love.

They grew tired of being chatted up
as though all a screaking hinge dreamt
of was being gatecrashed. I know that love's
a guttered-candle green, nothing but ends.

When really what does a screaking hinge dream?
The ha-ha of enchant and garble's what.
Each gunned blue, yellow, green. No end. Endless.
The bridesmaids have gone paintballing.

Barmbrack

Mother of God,
two houseflies were making love
on what must have been their honeymoon.
My grandmother struck them with a dishcloth.
The dirty fuckers, she said,
sweeping them into her open palm
like currants fallen from the barmbrack loaf
at the heart of which lay a golden ring.

Small Yellow Spider

I want to take you from that corner you like.
Closer, your figure, complicating the air.
Your invitation: to wonder what it's like, sightless,
the heart, bloody muscle, humming
through your wires. The blind brush of your leg
my thrill. In the end you may not want me.

Before bed I will forget to close the window.
Here's a good dark spot you can crash in. I'll lie
face up on the floor and the air gets tighter.
We will talk around our wants. We're modest.
I'll feel your hunger grow above me, and will wait
for you to sly down, bite my neck.

Pine Box in the Flea Market

The japanned pine box
with its cold brass handle and clasp
makes an enigma of the hall.
Opening it will be intimate, you think —
like the sudden glimpse of a heel
when she nips to the bath
leaving you and the bedposts to interpret
this new hush.

The box is burnished orange brown,
a finish the tint of Chilean Myrtle
or something choked with paprika,
with corners that could cut
like fishhooks. Watch your thumbs.
You want to poke about inside,
to shuck it open with an oyster knife,
spy in over the pine horizon,
and *whisht* you're saying *whisht* . . .

Inside? Maybe a bunch of shrunken heads;
a rosary of goats' teeth, bone blushing;
a pair of rusty, rubber-handled pliers;
the peekaboo of a tarantula —
you are a horsefly learning immensity
at the brink of a donkey's ear.

You can just picture shouldering it home
past bleeding candles, black veils,
mourners falling into step
and the shops closing on MacCurtain Street.
Someone clips a leash on his dog.

This is the clock's insomnia now —
your shoulder killing you all the way home
to a room on a numberless avenue
where blue snow is falling.

Polyphemus

He remembers the telescope most on winter nights —
a cheapish starter model, this, but it let him go
to Mare Imbrium and back in minutes;
then he's that nine-year-old who wheels it to the window,
tunes the sky, finds a keyhole in the hemisphere.
Sometimes the lens reflects only his myopic squints,
trained on whatever might chance to constellate
especially for his look — the soft blur
of the Pleiades, or Cassiopeia
he liked to picture rocking on a blue veranda;
or that god who, deaf to his charades, hints
nothing of himself and declines to comment
and is nobody's business for the moment
unless he means to say, *Sorry, you're too late.*

Interval (in which, snow)

Cool air surprises us awake,
has dried our puzzle
of bare limbs above the covers.
We must've drifted
after. Your bus due. Soonish.
In the interval, moon

I reckon by the light
but no. Snow is dicing down,
it settles and layers
and trapped voices carry
improbably far across
blinding gardens.

We get decent. I can't speak
much. At all. Anyway
snow damps our decibels,
arrests resonance
on this road we are
negotiating gingerly

down the middle.
We only overhear ourselves.
Just each other to
brace against
for traction. To lean
for painless purchase

on this earth and I cannot
walk you all the way.

Listening to Joni Mitchell's *Blue* While Cooking Peposo

More paint than accompaniment, your chords,
the day I held the yellowed Tuscan recipe
I'd chanced on, bent over charity shop shelves
in Bantry square. Your voice arose from blue –
I mean my Bluetooth pocket speaker, Spotified –
queued and looped and ringing fine as glass.
You sing: *the bed's too big, the frying pan's too wide*
but here is a shell for the blue. Who's Richard?
All ears, I seared cubed beef with garlic cloves,
a teacup of Chianti, black pepper in reckless dashes –
I chopped tomatoes gorgeous as her mouth
that sea-lit evening. And, though she didn't stay,
still your song moves through my kitchen at night.
It's 'California': *Will you take me as I am.*

Notes Toward an Epithalamium

All through the dinner
I kept schtum as a cup hook.
The exit was a matchbox lined
with false leaves and fishing
pleasantries. I poked at
a realistic shank of lamb,
admired the graphics of
the mashed potatoes. It was
just like being there except
I was. I excused myself
as often as decently possible
and then some. An ersatz peacock
exploded, all pearls and teeth.
The sommelier began evading
my eye. A halo made a pitstop
on Pap's cranium. Speech!
Toast strangers with empty glass.
Gracehopers on zimmerframes.
Mermaids lipsticking memoirs
on bathroom mirrors. You could
just break like a table leg.
The cheeses must endure such
leering, such inquisitions. Trifle
descends in merciless toboggans.
I wasn't made for these
situations. I'm not a person
who mingles easily. I'm not
a person, properly speaking.
Best wishes, whoever they are.

Pine Box in the Flea Market

after Vasko Popa, somewhat

The box grows.
It wants to be a tree again.
It misses being a tree.
It intends to be one again.
Or at least a larger box.

It opens its mouth —
on the red tongue
an old, bleached moth,
deathsung.

A Cigarette

You wouldn't *cadge* for starters, you'd bum or scab.
You'd pounce with 'last drag' or 'arse of that'.

A 'little rush of infinity' between school bells.
The Rizla peppered with what, Pap's Old Holborn

butterflied on the tripod of thumb and fingers,
a lick and a spark. We were cub initiates,

our scrum of lumpen uniforms on damp astro.
Last taker kept sketch for Nolan. His poncy whistle.

The roach, so bogged by then, would singe your lip
back to the bumfluff. In the blindspots of the new

CCTV, our uniforms smelt feral after light rain.
The mirrory, fluorescent slipstream

of the school corridors whispered with history,
the pale, class-portrait faces.

There was such gentleness in the architecture
of their hopes. They were friends.

I couldn't say where they are now, if still
hooked on the tonic blossom of that first sweet pull,

that burned awkwardly up one side,
cupped in inky fingers. Or didn't burn long.

Tabernacle

Castaways, we hit the forest – our camping stove
turned low, I gripped the tent close for its trial
in virgin attitudes of stiffness while
lamps fluttered on the dark. My roof sank wave
on wave accordion-like, the only sin
we knew; and soon the Jameson appeared.
I'd burned one back and by the third
she laid her hand on mine, like a napkin . . .

Later, I caught those tiny gasps from Joan
and Michael's tent where he slipped into her
like (this I thought) a frog à la Bashō;
those dark rippling walls where she kept centre,
held her breath, so I had to puzzle how
one could leave and neither be alone.

The Infinite

A sprig of mistletoe please
as I come nose to nose
with the abyss.

Prayer to Buster Keaton

Blessed Saint Buster, in the crispy reels I stream
you're stoic and all backbone, elastic as birch.
Bruises quadruple on set, but no wily switcheroos
for stunt doubles: you slick a tortoiseshell comb

across your quiff, tumble lamblike from the heights
(divorce, drink), trampoline back on fresh ground.
A cakewalk. And no poppy inflects the 'great stone face',
not farouche under the porkpie, more like a sieve

for liquid instants of feeling restrained in general . . .
Whether perched on a cowcatcher, shunting railroad ties
a sneeze from trainwreck – you were dangerous –
or that rooftop leap that went wrong. That went wrong

very right. It was an accident you let grow up.
Saint Buster, keep us from conniptions, keep us frisky
and adaptable on this path of fluke and gamble,
glorious fuck-ups I'll look back on and say, what luck!

Approach to an Egg

A boiled egg is a fresh beginning
and you tap the pale frangible shell
so delicately with the edge
of your spoon, you could be a convict

careful not to wake your cellmate
while you test the walls for weak spots,
brow glazed in response to a sun
rising the other side

Horse Chestnuts

Every September the horse-chestnuts appeared,
and it was oppressive, the weight
of new schoolbags, watched by those sticky burrs.
Soon a couple came unstuck,
falling along the margins of the road on which we played.
Others bruised unsplit, or showed buck-
eyed openings that slowly lost
their shine, sunk rotting past reach in thorny briars.
I liked the clean oily look of them, the little ghost
of a birthmark, the burnished glow;
pierced and strung, knocking conkers
punctuated Pythagoras' theorem, the heresy of Galileo
and so on. We were oblivious.
Don't know how long before the alarm was raised
but, in the way of things, it leaked to us.
Runaways were unheard of in our village, abduction
a notion so alien to us
we might have imagined an alien.
My mam rang your mam rang his mam rang her mam.
Every man was a man behaving strange.
A mystery to puzzle on the palm,
every September the horse-chestnuts appeared.
A girl from Senior Infants, I heard,
vanished three days, just as though to the other side of the glass.
Soon a couple came unstuck.
Packed into cars, we were driven to school and back.
Our dinners, burnt or underdone.

We eyed openings, but slowly lost
interest as conker-battles gave way to first frost.
I've been trying to conjure her face,
the birthmark, a burnished glow
up at the hairline. The squeak in her falsetto.
A daisychain wound in her freckled hands on the grass
and so on. We were oblivious.
They kept hush-hush
at home, as if small agents of rumour didn't rule the schoolyard.
Runaways were unheard of in our village. *Abduction*:
the word sent a big white van
through the bedroom wall of each night,
as my mam rang your mam rang his mam rang her mam.
At one point I even felt to blame,
sat on the grass, pulling the heads off daisies.
Every September the horse-chestnuts appeared.
And it was oppressive, the wait.
Soon a couple came unstuck,
falling along the margins of the road on which we played.
Eyes, opening, slowly lost
their shine, sunk. Rotting past reach in thorny briars
the birthmark, the burnished glow,
pierced and strung. Knocking conkers
and so on, we were oblivious
don't know how long. Before the alarm was raised
runaways were unheard of in our village, abduction
a notion so alien to us
my mam rang your mam rang his mam rang her mam.
Every man was a man behaving strange.

Quiche

Pain is a basement café and all of us are scrubbing
our merciless scrub, said the lady in the bloody apron,
staring through me. I'd asked for a slice of quiche
with goat's cheese and my finger was frozen on the sneezeglass.

Either I can be your mentor or you can wear pyjamas,
the mechanic yelled over the racket in his garage
when I suggested egg-white was no substitute for glue.
He climbed under the hood, and hasn't come out since.

A fly on the wall is enough company for a lifetime,
my mother insisted, while I stood above her on a stool
tending that fuse box. She wore black all the time now.
She kept spilling Lucozade on the dachshund in her lap.

I was out in the shed, reaching back to oil the hinges
that held my wings in position. It was hot work.
The last hour will be our worst, my wife said, and when I soared
our children were quick red ants leading her from the scene.

My Last Consultation

Doctor, I give you the bruised fruit
of my torso. Touch and I will dent,
form an ugly brownish hollow. Tap
my knee for a reflex it will fly off
on adventures, barbacking in Prague,
torturing a rival's orchids, a silvery
flick of studded football boot by night,
heeling a white horse over the meadows,
crushing glass at a Jewish wedding, toeing
lifts on the motorway, a nomad, ankleflash . . .
Doctor, I'm just cheesewire you manipulate
to secure from ravenous, imagined foxes
your next omelette. It is raining in Cork,
in Dublin it is raining, one umbrella is
as effectual as five. Doctor it is raining
in my body. You'll catch your death.
Press your stethoscope to my chest,
do you not hear Bach's Partita No. 2
in D minor as performed inside a whale?
Doctor, I know, I know, I know . . .
Don't put all my baskets in one egg.
Don't put all my widgets in one fish.
I will mind the platform between the train
and the gap when I disembogue.
But nine stitches is not so much?
Doctor, I'm tired of this diaphanous façade
of hope but I am not ready yet

to do the obituary mambo. Every job
I've known has been take the shift
or get the shaft. I'm learning to shirk.
But managers haunt, with tall orders,
targets and figures, the imagination.
My anxiety is a born lepidopterist
and my colours flutter in the suffocating
cone of its palms, such a dusky capture
making ash of what was brightest in me.
Doctor, please do not prescribe Rilke.
I ask for your medical not your moral counsel.
When one poodle died, Schopenhauer
would replace it with a new poodle.
To each poodle he gave the same name:
Benedict Cumberbatch.
Doctor, put a name on this dog.
I ask for your scalpel not your scapulars.
You may think you are the donkey's monocle
but you are not even nunchucks.
You may think you are the glistening satin
on a radish, but your cow burns down
while you whisper sweet nothings to milk.
How soon sweet nothings turn
to snickersnee. Doctor, you're bleeding.
Your parrot's clearly microwaved.
It's more chichi than rococo, I agree.
Have you ever wondered, is it art?

Parachuting into the Volcano

Watching Werner Herzog document the rages of a live volcano,
his temporary camp between Mount Merapi and the Chicken Church

hugged by jungle on a chessboard square of Central Java: it's tense.
Hope he remembered to pack his Dante. *Love brought us to one death.*

Easy to be put in mind of that Krafft couple, their triangular marriage
to the volcano. As children we played on the edge of fires

and made a game of escape. Babies, how were we to know better?
Babies, our parents, I can't blame them. They were the age then we are now.

The church is *ictuilly mint to riprisint a coronated dove,*
his still small voiceover crosses between my ears. A lisp of ash.

Don't stray too close now, Werner. Hardly worth the sexy footage.
It's enough to feel the blood trumpeting down your boulevards.

Or if you must wind up barbequed along one of the infernal thoroughfares
pray it's like the Kraffts, your hand soldered to mine.

The Pineapple Massage

*after 'ASMR Binaural Pineapple Relaxation',
Ephemeral Rift*

This YouTube video of a guy massaging a bespectacled pineapple
with joke-shop nose, brushing its spiny leaves and knocking *hello*

hello tension hello recurrent twinge in the joint outcha come —
he whispers nothings to the fruit, whose day has been so long.

I've never seen food used like this and the algorithm knows —
the dry leaves crickle, he can feel doors opening in the rind

and it's as if I have slipped through one and listen from inside.
I am alone. Oh, I might have laughed at this before:

somewhere there is a man who comforts the people by means
of a pineapple. He schools the ear in his curriculum of touch.

Yeah, even when he produces that big kitchen knife and carves
past the leafy plume to consume his client chunk by chunk —

so the blade sinks inches from my ear and the air brightens
yellow with the summer pent inside and is palpable.

Synastry Chart

Others lost livelihoods on horses,
had noses broken at poker tables,
the cards scattered like feathers.
You gambled too, married your chance.

Apartment in a bohemian seaside town . . .
How you cooked naked after sex,
swam in the sea
and drank white Rioja under skylights!

Well, no. But on one side stood a kebab shop,
a graveyard on the other –
submerged and mossed-over tombs
about the size of a bedroom,

her chin tense on your shoulder
as you tossed garlic cloves in the pan
like a couple of dice,
or the astrologer's knuckles.

Approach to Chilli

I'm catching the back garden in a colander held up
to the kitchen window — catching, rather, the fierce green glare
that filters in. When I've had enough I turn, think:
if I took a hacksaw and cut up the kitchen table
piece by piece, at what point exactly would it cease

to be a table? Which leg if any contains essence of table?
This kills time. Soon you will be home from a late shift
and I'll have cooked us both a vicious chilli, spitting
with onion, tomato, the red and yellow peppers, lentils, beans,
dashed with paprika, cumin . . . too much habanero.

Now they're mingling, ready to have their tantrum
on our tongues. What's left but to uncork a *Côtes du Rhône*
and rearrange the sitting room, in my head? There is no
TV, so all the furniture points to the furniture.
I slug back a glass then, one by one, tip up the chairs.

The Cup

He drops the espresso pod in, folds down the hatch
and activates the whizz – an interval ensues of maybe
ten seconds, no more, but it suffices to reflect
apropos of nothing how quickly the unforeseen becomes
today. A light beard webs his Lenten hollows.

And how quickly that big touchless summer's shelved,
the way a painting might impart a sense of paintedness,
or a ghost of smell stale in the nose from
fishy weeping through gaps in a wicker creel, where
finned fruit lay stunned on the bank of how

many years back? Now the cup's up to the brim,
above the brim the magpies like the keys on baby pianos
yammer against the sky's mushroom shade of beige.
It's possible to feel: *yes, every piano should experience flight
once, yes, my pinkie will yet fit inside this hook.*

Flies

The flies kept manifesting *ex nihilo*.
Thought I was equipped with a good swatter
that would last forever. I was wrong.
This was inconvenient but not fatal.
The flipflop I weaponized was effective
and music, the slain corpses falling
like arpeggios on a glockenspiel
and that was a result. Loud about my ears,
settling in my hair, down which each of
my secret thoughts ran, I felt them frolic
and wanted to die. Why were flies
so officious in this town? Enough landed
upon my friend once to carry him off
over the roofs, like in a Chagall —
but I clapped them dead, and the ones
I couldn't kill I turned into metaphor.

Percy French

The dead pig brought me tremendous grief. Plumped down
on his side like a pink beanbag full of bones, prickly
flesh with its sparse, candied hackles in a jacket
of lard, and that little rogue eye. I rubbed him between
the ears. I almost expected the tail to uncoil and wag.
I didn't even pause to ask how he got into the apartment
four flights up then died on the kitchen's sticky lino
with guests due to arrive any second. Clinking wine bottles
and heel-clicks preceded them on the stairwell. I fetched
my carpenter's pencil quick and traced around the carcass, but
it just wouldn't take, the point kept skiing off. The party
let themselves in. 'Ope! We know what's following our canapés',
one smirked. 'Get that man out of my flat', I said, 'now'.
I'd loved that pig. I can't say in all our lives we actually knew
each other. Yet here he was, hard clay wadded about his trotters.
The gristly pleats of his torso flabbed like an accordion. So
I gathered his bulk in my arms, scrunched him up the best
I could, and played that song he liked.

Afternaut

A month since I returned from the moon –
you might have got my postcard.
If you could decipher English in
my *ciotóg* smudge, you'll know
it was down a sidestreet past a Bächerei,
where wind-snapped white washing
hung anyshape from the balconies.
I mistook some lingerie for squirrels,
a willowy shadow-struggle above lawns
across Reinickendorf. I might've added
my moon wasn't pocked by craters,
baked volcanoes, vaporized lakes.
Roads were paved plumb with cycle lanes
from Shawarma to *Schultheiss*.
I missed company of course,
the way a body might miss corners,
being lost in that bedside-and-wall space,
a fissure day drops through,
the sweet ruelle. To lie on, leave
the world unseen, dissolve, and forget
what somehow you didn't know
you knew you knew. Bedside, a bridge
you'd lean over in the night where
the fish slithy like intuition to
some weedy downstream address.
Garlic, and plenty of it in everything forever!
I'm in the kitchen with the music on,

cracking cloves from the provocative
bouquet on a chopping-board in Cork,
watched from the window by one star.
There were no corners on the moon,
but the nightingales were awesome
being altogether not there.
I scale back the skin with a thumbnail,
finely slice a crescent with the rest
and dance it in a skillet with bream.
Let the pungent Esperanto speak
from my pores for a week. Let the skin
be a scratchy module separating
on its way down to the Sea of Tranquillity
                    or maybe the Ocean of Storms.

Self-Checkout

He told me he got lost once
in the aisles of a Tesco Express –
not physically disorientated,
more as if a glitch occurred
in the escapement of a timepiece –
a wheel the size of a coffee bean
scooting loose, and all gravity
pressed down on that space.

All the apples fell there.
I think I know what he meant.
He'd left the gaff for celery
not an existential brouhaha.
Some days I know myself
only in the way you'd consume
a crisp green apple, keeping
distance from the core.

It is necessary to remember
the hardy grain of the table
in a kitchen in Aherlow,
how it spoke to your elbows:
I was once a seed
so minute you could swallow me
whole and not notice.
Lean on me, be nourished.

Reverb

i

The grandson I am knows
all about bleeding pig in the yard,
filching apples, auctioning
all but the rushy acres
of an inherited farm, being robbed,
conjuring brown trout
through bulrushes with the unlikeliest lure:
cheddar, chocolate.

How constellations marshal above fields humming with frost,
Orion, the Pleiades. The night mountains.
How they swallow the shadows.
Shoebox burials by moonlight in the *cillín*.

A great grandfather was from Aghnameadle, Tipperary.
A great grandmother from Knocknagoshel, Kerry.
A grandmother, their daughter, herself from Charleville, Cork,
arrived, via teashop shifts and dances in London,
in Aherlow, Tipp again, my navvy grandfather's place,
then my mother's. Then mine.

ii

I've heard that a horse's skull
strategically placed under floorboards
acted as an amplifier,
made ceilidhs more resonant
when fiddles sped, dancers
stamped rhythm. Add bottlecaps,
add coins, it became a tambourine.
How grey-haired grandchildren
found them, pulling up floorboards,
and held the skull of a horse as if
it was just the skull of a horse.

Party After The The

The basil plant scenting the window ledge. You could watch it
succumb for months. To a raffle of aphids. To heat.
You could take cuttings to garnish your bruschetta with sweet
contingency. You could love how to it it must seem
risible mooning after trumpet when all there is is
triangle. Ding. Flattened and blemished it laments nothing.
Spirited piecemeal from evergreen, no no. It cost you
two euros in the supermarket's godless fluorescence.
Why not sniff. Be late to the appointment sniffing.
It smells like old guitar dusted and restrung. Smells of yes
and meant. A modicum of some former *ah* restored.
It could charcoal fast here. You can't reverse
the herb's miniature demolition, but roll it round your gob
and wake your palate with mouthfuls of window. Of hinge.

The Goatfish

Tired of the new quiet and a cat hair
in the soup you never made as sweet as hers,
at the first cindery pipsqueak of dawn
you'll bestir yourself out into the woods
and live on robins' eggs and rainwater
from a stoup of birch bark, wrung from moss;
chanterelles, brandy-warm, in a lee of ash.
Like wandering Aengus, or like Orpheus
riffing under earth just to double the grief –
this thought teasing at your temples:
as though she might shake off soil and roses,
reappear, mobled in veils, glowing like foxfire,
visible from parish to sister parish, say:
the cut of you, la, and cups left in the sink?
Pack it in, Aengus, Orpheus, pipe down!
The world is more wide for your wandering.
Folding one sock into the other, or
kneeling to separate halm from rhubarb halm
in a straw hat, your ordinary is so strange
you might as well be filleting goatfish
on the far side of the moon – scraped scales
flying from you like a rash of Leonids. La.

As If, A Land Called

Revving against the glass,
this one bearded moth with grey-brown
biker patch on his grizzled wings.
His eye is on us. If he gets in
our world is ash —
clothes, curtains, with a flameless burnt-look
after the smudge of exhaust from
the thumb's-length engine
he is. He'd unstitch us
back to kidney-beans, love.
I want to be wrong about him of course.
Let's be wrong and imagine him
an emissary of some dreamt place where
stones float,
the pats of claggy spawn we scooped at the pond's edge,
as children, are splurging
themselves on themselves —
our Hy-Brasils, our Never-Nevers. Oh
swagger of windfall apples that
unrot and are restored
to dizzy office; how bad
to wander in error, as if inside
error, just to feel
the walls, the ceiling against your heels.

NOTES

'Pinball' is for Matthew Sweeney.

'Spacer': as reported by Bernard Clarke on *Blue of the Night*, RTÉ Lyric FM (who was told the anecdote by Brian Palm of the Mary Stokes Band), Byther Smith petitioned NASA to make him the first man to play the blues on the moon. He was entirely successful and is still there to this day.

'To Félicette': Félicette was a stray Parisian cat selected by scientists for the French space program. Known as 'C 341', she survived the proposed sub-orbital mission and on 18 October 1963 became the only cat to have ever gone to space. Two months later she was euthanised so that an autopsy could be performed, and her brain studied. The scientists later concluded that they had learned nothing of any use from this.

'Listening to Joni Mitchell's *Blue* While Cooking Peposo': italicised lines are from 'My Old Man' and 'California' respectively.

'A Cigarette': a 'little rush of infinity' is Richard Klein's phrase from *Cigarettes Are Sublime*, as quoted in Ciaran Carson's *Last Night's Fun*.

'The Infinite' is in memory of Charles Simic.

'Flies' is for Shane Forde.

'Parachuting into the Volcano': the italicised line derives from Dante's *Inferno*, canto 5 as translated by the Hollanders. Maurice and Katia Krafft were pioneering volcanologists who were killed in a pyroclastic flow on Mount Unzen, Nagasaki, Japan.

ACKNOWLEDGEMENTS

Acknowledgements are gratefully made to the following magazines where many of these poems first appeared: *Banshee, Bath Magg, Cheerio, Columbia Review, The Irish Times, The London Magazine, New York Review of Books, The North, Winter Papers, Poetry London, Poetry Magazine, Poetry Ireland Review, The Poetry Review, The Tangerine, Southword, The Stinging Fly.*

Some of these poems were published in *Kitchens at Night*, a winner of the Poetry Business International pamphlet competition (Smith|Doorstop, 2022). Also in limited edition pamphlets *Tracing Ogham* (O'Bheal, 2022) and *Lunch Poems* (Listowel Writers Week, 2023).

'My Last Consultation' won the Geoffrey Dearmer Prize, 2021.

Special thanks to Michael Dooley, Scott McKendry and Tom Moore who engaged with these poems at various stages, and to poet friends for advice and encouragement, among them Harry Bradley, Ben Burns, Cal Doyle, Daniel Fraser, John Mee, Mary Noonan, Billy Ramsell, Maurice Riordan, Keith Payne.

And to Paul Casey of O'Bheal and Patrick Cotter of the Munster Literature Centre for generosity and invitations over the years.

I gratefully acknowledge vital support from the Arts Council of Ireland, the Tipperary County Council, and the Basic Income for the Arts pilot scheme, which made possible the completion of this work.

I am grateful to my agent Angelique Tran Van Sang and to the Picador crew, Ebruba Abel-Unokan, and Colette Bryce for her keen eye and grounded wisdom in guiding this collection.

Love to Laura, my closest reader.